All about Knights

For over 600 years the medieval knight dominated the battlefields and politics of Europe. By what means did he train and equip himself for this supreme role? How good were his ideals, sports, castles and horses? Why did the knightly way of life die out? These questions and many more are answered in this richly illustrated and expertly written ALL COLOR FACT BOOK.

Contents

The Rise of the Knight

The European Middle Ages between 800 and 1450 A.D. were dominated by the knight. In war, he was a skilled fighter and an armored horse-soldier. In peacetime, he was a landowner and a ruler of men. The knight appeared at a time of great violence and bloodshed when Western Europe was being attacked by the Vikings from Scandinavia in the North and West; by the Arabs from Africa in the South and by the Magyars from the steppes of Asia in the East. The forefathers of the men who defended Europe against these fierce, ruthless invaders had seized their lands from the Romans some centuries earlier. Now it was the turn of the medieval Europeans to stand and defend these same countries.

The Europeans' main weapon against the invaders was horse-soldiers or cavalry. The idea of cavalry was not a new one. The Ancient Greeks and Romans had used horse-soldiers but they had never taken the place of their heavily armed foot-soldiers, or infantry, because they could not charge the packed ranks of the enemy's foot-soldiers effectively. Before cavalrymen could come into operation as a military unit, they needed some kind of support for their feet, in other words stirrups.

Before the invention of stirrups, cavalrymen had the greatest difficulty fighting on horseback. If they wore heavy armor, they were likely to lose their balance. If they charged their enemies with their spears extended in front of them, they were likely to be swept from the saddle by the impact of their spears hitting heavy bodies. But with stirrups attached to the saddle by long leather straps so that their legs were straight, medieval knights were able to do combat sitting firmly in their saddles.

Although historians think that stirrups were invented in China at the end of the fifth century A.D., news of their use took a long time to reach the West. In fact, the Europeans seem to have known nothing about them until the reign of Charlemagne, the king of the Franks (742–814), who ruled France

Right: The Battle of Hastings. The Anglo-Saxons met their match when they left their position on Senlac Hill. The Norman cavalry cut them to pieces as soon as they reached the plain.

Below: For many years historians thought that knights rode huge destriers like modern shire horses, but research has shown that their war-horses were much more like the Morgan horse pictured here.

many and northern Italy. Even
—, we do not know how the idea
—ntually reached the Franks. Some
—orians think that the Franks
—ned about stirrups while they were
—nding their country from the
—bs, who had already invaded Spain.
—nce the Europeans started using
—ups, other developments followed
—dly. Long pointed shields were
—gned to cover the whole of the
—y and cavalrymen learned to
—op at top speed into their enemies
— stab them with their spears
—ead of throwing them. Their

horses were shod with metal shoes so
that they could travel over the
roughest ground without splitting
their hooves. It was now possible for
a rider to wear heavy armor
without losing his balance when
leaning forward or backward. This
was because he was able to stand up
in the saddle by letting down his
leather stirrup straps until his legs
were at full stretch.

These changes amounted to a
military revolution. For the time
being the day of the infantryman was
over and the day of the cavalryman

or knight had come. As a knight's
armor and war-horse were so
expensive some means of paying for
them had to be worked out. Instead
of hiring and equipping ordinary
soldiers, the medieval kings
preferred to give away part of their
lands to their followers. These men
governed the estates for their king
and supplied him with soldiers
whenever he needed them. This
brought into being a new system of
landholding. It is now called the feudal
system and it produced a new kind of
soldier, the knight.

The Feudal System

Under the feudal system in some parts of Europe only the king owned land and all other noblemen were tenants. During the eighth and ninth centuries, some kings of Western Europe divided up many of their lands among their leading followers: the counts and barons. These men became their chief tenants or *tenants-in-chief*. As the lands of the tenants-in-chief were so extensive, they in turn loaned or gave some of their land to their followers, who were called *mesne-tenants* or lesser tenants.

In return for his estates, each tenant or *vassal* knelt before his lord, placed his hands between those of his lord and promised to serve him faithfully and provide him with military help. This ceremony was called *homage* and the promise was called the *oath of fealty*. By this oath, the tenant was expected to arm and mount himself and be ready to fight when his lord needed him. All tenants-in-chief were expected to provide the king with a certain number of armed men, depending upon the size of their estates. The tenants-in-chief raised knights from their mesne-tenants in the same way.

As a result, these soldier-farmers or knights became a military class whose way of life was dominated by war and preparations for war. Even the bishops who received royal land were expected to supply the king with soldiers and some of them even fought for him in person. These men of the Church armed themselves with clubs or maces with which they beat their opponents to death. By using these weapons they technically obeyed Church law which forbade them to shed blood.

The feudal lords had tremendous power over the ordinary people, the *villeins*, who lived on their estates. The villeins had to pay them taxes, work on their land for two or three days a week, and give them

Below: Torture was sometimes used to extract confessions. Convicted criminals were displayed in open carts.

ht and below: This pyramid
...ws the basic structure of
...feudal system. Each of the
...itary classes, the barons and
...hops and the knights, swore
...hs of fealty to their superiors,
...the chief lord had no superior.
...ne peasants were the property
...he military classes and could
...ought and sold.

...ow left: Most peasants had to
...rk on the land belonging to
...ir lord of the manor. Certain
...sants were specialists. Some
...e shepherds, cattleherds or
...tasters. Shown here is a
...utiful picture of a peasant
...aring sheep.

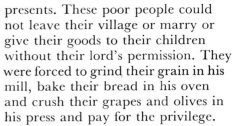

presents. These poor people could
not leave their village or marry or
give their goods to their children
without their lord's permission. They
were forced to grind their grain in his
mill, bake their bread in his oven
and crush their grapes and olives in
his press and pay for the privilege.

Most great feudal lords in France
and Germany possessed the right of
High Justice. This meant they could
hang villeins found guilty of stealing
or murdering. In England, things
were slightly different. The feudal
lords were allowed only the right of
Middle or Low Justice. Those who
had the right of Middle Justice
could hang tenants if they found
stolen goods on their property. The
holders of Low Justice were only
allowed to put people in the stocks or
have them whipped.

A good lord ruled his tenants justly
and protected them against robbers
and invaders. A bad lord treated his
people cruelly and made their lives
miserable. A successful feudal state
was one where the king was so
respected by his followers that they
kept their oaths of fealty and
remained loyal. This produced a
well-organized country that could
defend itself against any enemy.
However, when the king's followers
were disloyal the whole structure of
feudalism fell apart and resulted in
civil wars and invasions. As their
country was small, most of the
medieval kings of England managed
to control their nobles. Unfortunately,
there were also some very bad
rulers, such as Stephen (1097-1154),
Henry III (1207-72), Edward II
(1284-1327), Richard II (1367-
99) and Henry VI (1421-71). On the
other hand, the French kings had the
greatest difficulty ruling their large
country. Some of their great vassals
such as the king of England, who,
until 1204, was also duke of Normandy,
count of Anjou-Maine and duke of
Aquitaine, were as powerful as they
were. The French nobles continued
to challenge their kings in the 16th
and 17th centuries long after the
Middle Ages were over.

The Page - a Military Apprentice

In the Middle Ages, some of the boys destined to become knights trained from early childhood in the knightly arts. The first stage in their military apprenticeship was served as a page in a noble's household. A page learned not only about military matters but also about honor and courteous behavior, especially toward women.

The son of a knight spent his earliest years with his nurse and the other women in the castle. During this time, he learned something about manners and how to behave. Sometimes he was taught to read but rarely to write. In addition, he started to learn to sing and play a musical instrument. The turning point in his life came when he was given his first pony. He was taught to look after horses and to ride them expertly.

When he was about seven or eight, he was sent away from home to be a page at the court of the king or some great lord. A page's main duties were to run errands, help the lady of the household with her duties, learn to come when he was called and to wait patiently when there was nothing for him to do. As he grew older he was trained in the use of weapons, especially the sword and bow. He learned to handle a lance by *tilting at the quintain*. The *quintain* was an upright post with a pivoted crossbar. There was a shield on one end of the bar and a heavy sack on the other. The idea was for the page to ride full speed or *tilt* at the quintain, hit the shield a resounding blow with his lance and duck under the swinging sack. The unfortunate beginner was usually swept out of the saddle time after time by the swinging sack, but this was all part of the training.

The page also started to learn the art of *venery* or hunting. He had to be able to recognize the *spoor* (the footmarks) and the *fewmets* (the droppings) of the forest animals so that he could track them to their lairs. To find his way safely through dense forest, he had to know how to follow and leave a trail.

Above: Hunting was regarded as the ideal preparation for war. It required quick wits to deal with unexpected developments. The wild boar was one of the most dangerous animals hunted by medieval people. What other animals are being hunted in this picture and the one below?

Right: A lanner falcon rests up its master's glove. The falcon's feet are its main weapon. These talons grip the prey while the razor-sharp beak rips it to piec When not hunting, the falcon w kept hooded (see above) and wo bells attached to its feet. A page had to be familiar with falconr

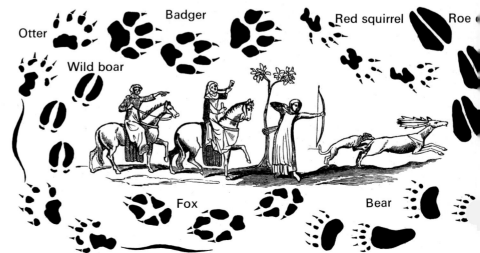

Above: A page learned how to handle a lance by riding at the quintain. The lance was flexible and wavered as he rode forward. He only gripped the shaft tightly at the last moment. He aimed at the shield on the crossbar.

Medieval men admired the courage and faithfulness of their dogs. There were nearly as many different types then as there are today, such as watch-dogs, sheep-dogs, guard dogs and hounds of all kinds, as well as pet dogs. Each lord had a dogboy who lived with the hounds in their kennels, learned their characteristics and looked after them in every way. The page, too, had to know the ways of dogs so that he could get the best out of them when hunting.

A knowledge of falconry and hawking was also part of his education. Falcons and hawks are birds of prey which can be taught to hunt game for their masters. Medieval falconers trained their hunting birds to come to a *lure* (a dummy bird containing a piece of meat) which was whirled around on the end of a piece of rope. Except during hunting, these fierce birds were kept hooded and had tiny bells attached to their legs so that their every movement could be heard.

Pages spent a good deal of their time hunting or waiting upon the huntsman. Anything that could run or fly was hunted by the members of the knightly class with the greatest enthusiasm.

7

The Squire-a Knight in Training

At about the age of 14 if the page had made satisfactory progress he became a squire and, if he belonged to, or served in, a wealthy family, he put on silver spurs as a sign of his new status. As a squire, he had the right to carry a shield emblazoned with armorial bearings and to wear a helmet like a knight's.

At this stage of his training, he was placed with a knight who continued his education and treated him as a kind of companion and general servant. A good deal of his time was spent cleaning his own and his master's armor. He also helped his knight to dress and undress, made his bed and looked after his clothes. Each evening he took him a glass of spiced wine and slept across the doorway to his bedchamber to protect him from sudden attack.

As a knight in training, the squire learned to leap into the saddle without touching the stirrups and to guide his horse by pressing its flanks with his knees and heels. He built up his strength by wrestling and running and jumping. He practiced wielding his heavy weapons until he could fight for long periods without becoming exhausted.

At the opening of tournaments, the squire rode before his knight, holding his helm in his left hand and his tilting lance in his right. If his knight was successful, the squire guarded his prisoners until they were ransomed.

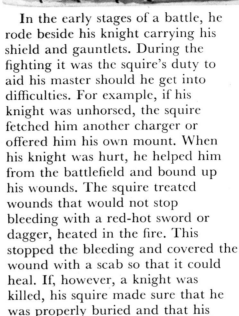

In the early stages of a battle, he rode beside his knight carrying his shield and gauntlets. During the fighting it was the squire's duty to aid his master should he get into difficulties. For example, if his knight was unhorsed, the squire fetched him another charger or offered him his own mount. When his knight was hurt, he helped him from the battlefield and bound up his wounds. The squire treated wounds that would not stop bleeding with a red-hot sword or dagger, heated in the fire. This stopped the bleeding and covered the wound with a scab so that it could heal. If, however, a knight was killed, his squire made sure that he was properly buried and that his master's feudal lord was informed.

As a member of the noble class, the squire was expected to learn the arts of civilized behavior. He had to be able to make conversation and to entertain his master's guests. He learned to play checkers, chess and other games. If he wanted to be a social success he had to be able to

dance, sing and play music skilfull A gallant young man, such as the squire in Geoffrey Chaucer's *Canterbury Tales*, dressed in the hei of fashion with a fine tunic that w embroidered all over with red and white flowers and had long, wide sleeves. Such an elegant young ma could hope to catch the eyes of the ladies. Chaucer (1340-1400) slyly remarked that his squire loved so hotly that he slept as little as a nightingale.

By the time a squire reached the age of 21, he was qualified to becc a knight. However, he could only advance to this honor if he had sufficient land or money to enable him to carry out the duties of a knight. As a result, many squires never achieved knighthood.

The Knighting Ceremony

Above: Three knights having their swords buckled on. This was the greatest moment in the life of every medieval knight.

Above: During the night of Vigil, the priest reminded the squire that it was his duty to serve God before all men. His weapons were blessed while he prayed. In the morning, he confessed his sins to the priest.

Although knighting had been a simple affair during the early Middle Ages, the ceremony gradually became more and more complicated. By the end of the Middle Ages, it was performed in the grounds before some great castle amid great celebrations.

On the day before the knighting ceremony (known as *dubbing*) took place, the squires had their hair cut short to remind them that they should humble themselves in the eyes of God. In those days, a man regarded his hair as his best feature or crowning glory. Then, they bathed to show that their sins were being washed away and that they were about to start a new life. After that they put on black shoes and lay on their beds. The fact that the shoes were black, the color of death, reminded them that they would die

one day and the bed which provided comfort and rest reminded them they would rest in Heaven if they lived up to the ideals of knighthood.

The squires then recited the laws of chivalry. Although there was no particular code of rules, the following points are a fair summary of the things that knights were supposed to believe in and live up to: a knight was required to obey God's teachings; defend the Church; protect the weak and helpless; fight for his native land; never retreat before an enemy; wage ceaseless war on non-Christians; always obey his feudal lord; and always support good against evil.

Above: An unworthy knight is hauled through the streets. He is being publicly disgraced for breaking the rules of his order.

ow: The knighting of squires
he field of battle became more
more unusual by the later
dle Ages. Most squires
owed an elaborate course in
ghtly studies before being
ghted with great ceremony.

After this the squires attended a banquet where they ate their fill. It was the last food they were to have for many hours. That night they entered the castle chapel and laid their weapons on the altar so that they could be blessed by the priest. The squires spent the rest of the night in the chapel praying. This part of the ceremony was called the *Vigil at Arms* and it reminded the squires that they should only use their weapons in God's service.

At last the great moment arrived and the squires filed out onto the green lawns before the castle where a huge crowd was eagerly waiting to see the climax of the ceremony. Each squire advanced in turn and had his sword buckled on by one knight and his beautiful golden spurs by another. Then the most senior knight present came forward and gave the squire a cuff on the neck or a light blow on the shoulder with a sword to show that the squire was now a knight. This was known as the giving of the *accolade*.

Of course, many squires were dubbed knight in far less romantic circumstances. Many received the accolade on the field of battle surrounded by their dead and dying comrades. Although squires were usually knighted by people who were not related to them, fathers sometimes dubbed their own sons. No matter who conferred the honor or where the ceremony took place, this was the greatest honor any medieval soldier could receive.

A Knight and his Armor

As we have seen, the invention of the stirrup enabled horse-soldiers or knights to wear heavy armor and, at the same time, to control their horses in battle. By the 11th century, knights were almost completely covered in *mail* armor. Mail was made of small interlocking steel rings so that each ring had four others linked through it. Together they made a fabric strong enough to protect the wearer from most cutting blows. Each armor or *harness*, as a suit of mail was called, had to be properly planned. The knight had to be carefully measured to make sure that his armor fitted him perfectly. As mail was very expensive to make, it was usually passed down from father to son and modified by the family

armorer to fit the new wearer.

Mail was not nearly as heavy as it sounds. Indeed, it was probably about as heavy as the equipment worn by a modern infantryman. A very strong knight, such as the Englishman William the Marshal (1152-1219), could dance in full mail. Nevertheless, a knight had considerable difficulty arming himself and really needed the help of his squire or a servant.

Below: First of all, he put on line stockings, breeches and a long sleeved shirt made of wool. On top of these clothes, he wo a leather tunic or a padded co called an *aketon;* this stopped h shoulders from being rubbed raw by the movement of the coat of mail.
Sometimes, the knight had to pull his *hauberk* or coat of mail over his head and wriggle insi but some hauberks were split the back so that the knight cou push his arms into the sleeves before his squire laced him in. Some knights wore mail leggir or *chausses.* The tops of these w attached by straps to a waist be to keep them up.

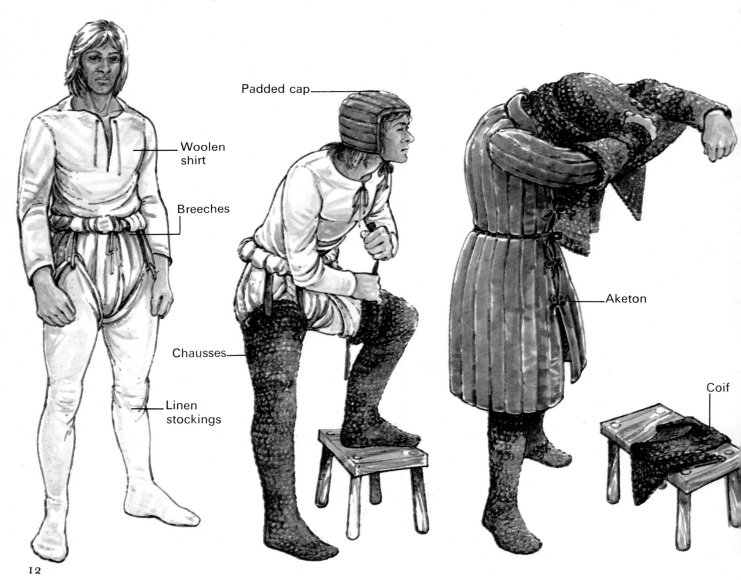

Padded cap

Woolen shirt

Breeches

Chausses

Linen stockings

Aketon

Coif

if, a king of chain mail
...d, was pulled over the head
...d hung down over the neck
...d shoulders.

...imple conical helmet made of
...ther or metal, which was
...ded like a modern crash
...met to protect the head from
...vy blows, was worn on top of
... coif. A strip of metal called a
...l guarded the nose from
...rdcuts across the face. A
...ple type of spur, known as a
...k *spur* was buckled into place
...each foot.

...e knight's equipment was
...pleted by a long, heavy
...rd in a *scabbard* or *sheath*, and a
...ge kite-shaped shield held
...lace by leather straps.

Conical helmet

Nasal

Hauberk

Prick spur

Hoïe a man schaff be armyd at his efe
whßen he schal fighte on foote

Æe schal haue noo schute up on him but a
doublelet of ffustean lyuyd with satene cutte
full of hooßs. the doublelet muste be stronglech bonde

Above: Notice that the squire
has laid out his master's armor
in a sequence so that it can be
put on with speed and ease. Every
piece of armor had to be buckled,
screwed or tied in position to
ensure a comfortable fit.

Below: Armorers usually
specialized in certain techniques.
Some shaped the metal, some
fitted rivets and hinges and some
decorated the finished armor.
The making of armor required
great skill.

From Mail to Plate Armor

Below: By the 13th century, a knight's armor had changed in many ways. Most knights had mail mittens (1) at the end of the sleeves of their hauberk (2). These were split along the palms so that the hands could be freed without taking off the rest of the armor. Helmets called *flat-topped helms* (3) became fashionable and a new lozenge-shaped shield (4) came into use. Many knights took to wearing linen tunics called *surcoats* (5) which were slit up the back and front to make riding easier. The Crusading knights found these surcoats particularly useful in the Holy Land as they shielded their armor from the sun and helped to keep them cool. Moreover, the knight's coat-of-arms could be displayed on his surcoat so that everyone knew who he was.

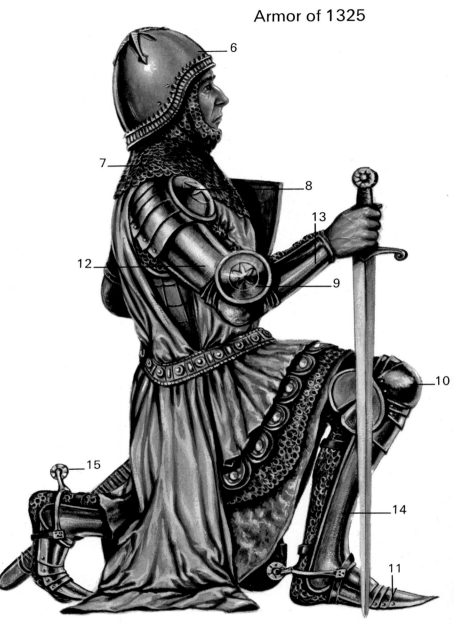

Armor of 1325

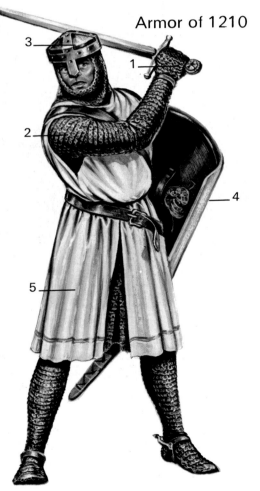

Armor of 1210

Above: During the 14th century, a new kind of helmet or *helm* called a bascinet was introduced. It was a metal skull cap and an elaborate helm (6) could be placed over it. A heavy cape of mail called an *aventail* (7) hung down from the bottom of the helmet to protect the neck and shoulders. The armpits were protected by *roundels* (8), the elbows by *couters* or *elbow-kops* (9), the knees by *poleyns* or *knee-kops* (10) and the feet by *solerets* (11). The upper arms were enclosed in plate armor called *rerebraces* (12), the lower arms by *vambraces* (13) an the legs by *schynbalds* (14).

All these pieces of plate armor were held in place by straps a buckles and were worn over t top of a suit of mail. At this time, the prick spur was replaced by the *rowel spur* (15) an the lozenge-shaped shield by a flat-iron-shaped shield. This ki of armor was worn at the battl of Crécy which was fought betv the English and the French in 1346.

Armor of 1415

Below: By the 16th century the greatest days of working armor were over and yet this was the time when the finest harnesses were made. Splendid close-fitting helms called *armets* (21) were worn while the breast and back plates were perfectly molded to fit the shape of the wearer's body. Thigh protectors called *taces* (22) were added to the fauld and the head and shoulders were defended by raised *haute pieces* (23). By this time a shield was rarely used so that the left pauldron was reinforced with a large plate while the neck was surrounded by a metal *beaver* (24). The arms and legs were completely encased in armor.

Armor of 1548

ove: By the time of the battle gincourt in 1415, whole suits late armor were available. cinets with *visors* of the ndskull type (16) were worn. ast and back plates protected upper part of the body. The er part was defended by a ies of thin plates called a d (17). The joints were given

even more protection as you can see by the size of the *pauldrons*, (18), *coudes* (19) and *genouillères* (20). Notice that the knight still wore mail underneath his plate armor. The greatest weakness of this kind of armor was that the wearer could not turn his head to see behind him as his helmet was fixed.

Weapons of the Middle Ages

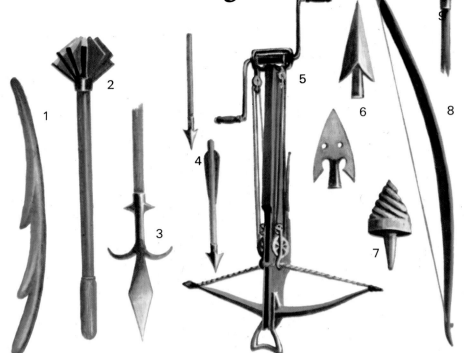

Knights were men of the sword. Their iron blades were heated, cooled and hammered many times before they became steel. Their blades were often damascened, that is inlaid with gold and silver designs. The knight held the sword by the *hilt* which was protected by two guards called *quillons*. The *pommel*, a large knob at the end of the hilt helped balance the blade. A longsword weighed between three and five pounds and was used for cutting, slashing and occasionally thrusting. When not in use, it was carried in a scabbard. In battle, the longsword was usually attached to the knight's breastplate by a thin chain so that it could not be lost.

The lance was made of ash, pine or some other wood and was between 8 and 15 feet long with a conical, triangular or lozenge-shaped point. By the 14th century proper hand grips and guards were added and an iron spike or *ferrule* was fitted to the butt so that the lance could be stuck in the ground. If a knight grounded his lance, it was a sign that he wanted to talk or *parley* with his opponent.

In addition every knight had secondary weapons such as the battle-axe, the mace or the war-flail. The battle-axe was a formidable weapon. At the battle of Bannockburn in 1314, Robert the Bruce of Scotland (1274-1329) was attacked by a young English knight. As the Englishman dashed forward the Scottish king rose in his stirrups and smashed his battle-axe down on the knight's head, almost cutting it completely in two.

Maces were clubs with spikes or flanged heads. They were sometimes called "holy water sprinklers" because they were used by priests in battle. The war-flail was even more frightening. It consisted of a spiked iron ball on the end of a chain connected to a handle and was used to bludgeon opponents.

The foot-soldiers' main weapons were longbows and crossbows. Knights would use neither in battle believing them to be unknightly weapons. The longbow was made of strong, supple yew. A notch was cut in both ends of the stave so that a length of hemp could be strung between them. Both the bow and string were waxed and resined to keep them in good condition. The arrow or *clothyard* was about one yard long and was armed with a metal head. Broad heads were used against foot-soldiers and thin bullet-like heads against armored knights. The arrows were flighted with split quill feathers.

Crossbows, which were introduced in the 11th century, were made of wood or horn. After shooting, the string was drawn back by the archer placing his foot in the stirrup. He then attached the string to a hook in his belt and straightened his back until the string slipped over the retaining catch on the crossbar of the weapon. The bow was usually shot by means of some kind of trigger. Later a geared contrivance called a windlass was used to wind back the string. Crossbows shot short wooden or iron arrows called bolts or *quarrels*. Although much slower to load than the longbow, the crossbow was a powerful and accurate weapon.

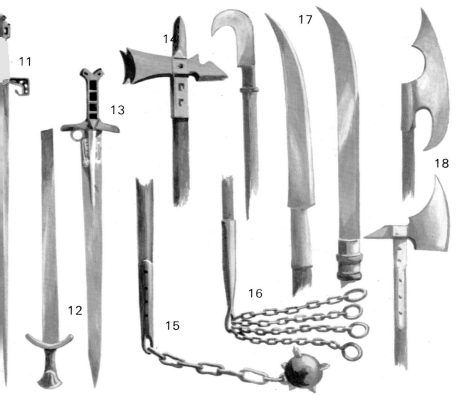

Left: A selection of medieval hand weapons: 1. Norman mace; 2. English mace; 3. Halberd; 4. War crossbow bolts; 5. Crossbow with windlass; 6. Barbed arrowheads; 7. Screw arrowhead; 8. Longbow; 9. Jousting lance-head; 10. War lance-head; 11. German sword; 12. English sword; 13. German sword; 14. War-hammer; 15. Military flail; 16. German scorpion; 17. War scythes; 18. Pole-axes.

Below: A battle scene from the later Middle Ages. See how many different weapons you can spot. There are longbows, crossbows, swords, daggers, lances and cannon. Successful cannon were produced in the 14th century.

Coats-of-Arms

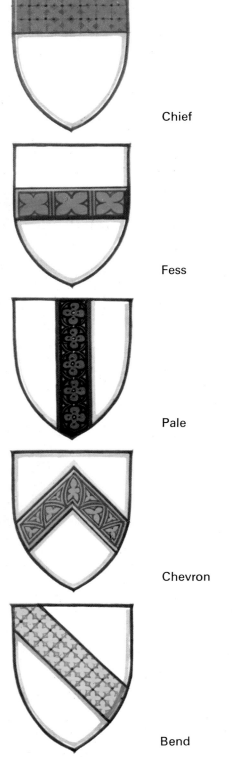

Below: The figures or shapes on a heraldic shield were called charges. The oldest and simplest charges were the *ordinaries*. Here are five typical examples.

Chief

Fess

Pale

Chevron

Bend

Heraldry dates from the second half of the 12th century. There were no coats-of-arms at the time of the First (1096-99) and Second (1147-49) Crusades. Medieval heraldry was a system of identifying people by means of signs or pictures, usually depicted on a shield. The need for this kind of identity arose because the helmet covered so much of a knight's face it was impossible to recognize him. In order to be recognized, each knight wore a surcoat marked with his family's colors and symbols. This was his coat-of-arms.

The whole coat-of-arms was called an *achievement*. This consisted of a personal shield, crest, helmet, mantling, wreath and motto. The shield was the most important item as it carried the coat-of-arms of the individual knight. The crest was a small model of an animal or bird made of boiled leather and worn on top of the helmet. The mantling was a cloth cape worn over the back of the helmet to stop the wearer getting sunstroke. The wreath was a circle of silk and gold or silver cord twisted around the helmet to cover the joint between the mantling and the crest. The motto was a short phrase or saying. However, not every

Label

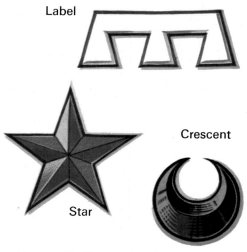

Crescent

Star

Above: Cadency marks distinguished a father's coat-of-arms from his sons': a label for the eldest, a crescent for the second; a star for the third.

achievement had all these items. I fact some of the oldest achievemen consisted of the shield alone.

The surface of the shield was called the *field* and the figures or shapes on it were *charges*. Shields could be of various shapes but the flat-iron shape was the most popul It was usually shown in the uprigh position but it could be sloping.

The field and charges were colored. The colors or *tinctures* were either two metals: *argent* (silver) and *or* (gold); or six colors: *sable* (black), *azure* (blue), *gules* (r vert (green), *tenné* (orange), and *purpure* (purple).

The oldest charges, or the *ordinaries*, were the simplest: a bar across the top of the shield was called the *chief*; a bar across the middle was the *fess*; a bar down the middle was the *pale*; an upside dow v-shaped bar was the *chevron* and a diagonal bar was the *bend*.

Coats-of-arms were hereditary which meant they were passed fro parent to child. However, because two individuals could wear identi coats-of-arms at the same time, a special mark had to be used to distinguish each child from the father. In the case of the sons this was done by adding *cadency* marks the father's arms. The eldest son represented by a label, the second son by a crescent, the third by a star, and so on.

Wives and daughters were also allowed coats-of-arms. They displayed their husband's or father's achievement but in the fo of a lozenge instead of a shield an without a helmet, crest and mantling. Daughters could contin to use their father's arms after marriage. Usually, however, they impaled their arms with those of their husband. This meant the shi was divided per pale with the wife achievement on one side and the husband's on the other. In this way achievements became more and m complicated and, in some cases, it possible to trace a family's history from their achievement.

Some coats-of-arms changed as a result of marriages between their holders and heiresses. The illustration shows how a coat-of-arms changed as a result of three great marriages. The knight at the foot of the tree carries a shield which has been divided into four. The quarters bear the coats-of-arms the knight has inherited.

The Tournament

The first tournaments or mock battles were held in the tenth or eleventh century. From the very beginning, they were opposed both by the Pope, the head of the Roman Catholic Church, and the kings of Europe who objected to so many of their knights being badly wounded and even killed in this sport. In spite of all opposition, however, the tournament flourished and became an essential part of the knight's life.

The tournament started out as a simple contest between knights and gradually became more and more complicated and expensive. In its heyday, the tournament was a very exciting affair. A mass of tents was set up on level ground outside a great castle or town and people crowded from far and near to attend. The *lists* or fighting area were surrounded with gaily decorated stands for the spectators and pavilions where the knights taking part lived for the duration of the tournament.

Outside the pavilions the contestants hung up their shields. The competitors then issued challenges by riding up to a rival's shield and hitting it with either the butt or the point of their lance. If the challenger used the butt, it was a sign that he wished to take part in a *jouste à plaisance* or a friendly contest. On the other hand, if he used the point, he was challenging his opponent to a *jouste à l'outrance*, or a fight to the death.

When all was ready, there was a fanfare of trumpets then the heralds, the referees and judges of the contests, marched forward and read out the rules of the tournament and the military records of the knights taking part. There were several kinds of contest. The tournament proper was a mock battle when knights took on all comers. Although it often broke down into a series of single combats, it was not unusual for four or five knights to set about one famous competitor. Regular jousting contestants often made arrangements with other knights to come to their aid in these circumstances. When a knight was defeated, he became the property of the victor and had to pay a ransom,

Below: This medieval picture shows two knights jousting outside a city. See if you can work out the date from the styl of armor. Notice the fancy cres on the helmets. The horses are wearing linen or leather caparisons.

20

usually his armor or horse, to free himself.

The mêlée was a very dangerous form of mock battle between groups of rival champions. The contestants often became over-excited and in their enthusiasm wounded and even killed their opponents.

By far the most exciting contest was the jousting which was a knock-out competition when the competitors fought a series of single combats with lance, sword, battle-axe and mace. Special blunted weapons were used and there were strict rules. Points were taken off for missing a stroke, for wounding an opponent's horse, for hitting an opponent below the belt or when his back was turned and for striking him with the shaft of the lance instead of the point. The object of each combatant was to knock his opponent out of the saddle or to tear off his helmet. Each pair of knights rode between six and eight rounds.

Jousting could be a highly dangerous sport. Henry II of France (1519-59) was mortally wounded during a tournament to celebrate his daughter's wedding. The king, who was very proud of his skill, insisted on taking part in the jousting. In the final round, he was faced by Count Montmorency, the Captain of the Guard. When the two clashed, their spears splintered. The shattered ends of Montmorency's passed through the king's visor and penetrated his brain. Henry took 11 agonizing days to die.

...w: A mêlée was a mock battle ...een groups of champions. ...t started out as a friendly ...est often ended in real ...dshed. In the confusion of the ...ting, men were trampled to ...h; others were smothered in ...dust.

Above left: A tournament was a free fight. Each knight defended himself against all comers.

Above right: A joust was a personal contest between two knights. Sometimes they used blunt weapons.

Life in a Medieval Castle

The castle was not only a knight's home but also a sign of his power because a castle dominated the countryside around it. Castles were built all over Western Europe. Many were constructed on the kings' orders but far more were erected by their nobles. Most medieval kings were very unhappy about this as it meant that disloyal barons could defy them from the safety of these great fortifications. It was not until later, during the 14th and 15th centuries, after the development of gunpowder and the heavy siege gun which could batter down even the thickest walls, that castles began to lose their military importance.

The earliest castle was built as a place of safety in which a man could defend his family and servants. It was probably no more than a stone or wooden tower surrounded by earth ramparts and wooden fences. However, the 11th century saw the development of the stronger stone castle. At its center lay the keep or living quarters which stood in a spacious courtyard defended by curtain walls. During the 12th century, these walls were strengthened with square and round towers which enabled the defenders to see out over the surrounding countryside and shoot down at their attackers without being seen.

The castle was a world of its own containing stables, kennels, mews, bakeries, smithies and stores of all kinds. During the early Middle Ages, the lord and his lady, their knights and their servants lived in the keep. This great building with its huge thick walls and tiny glassless windows must have been both cold and dark. The main living room, the Great Hall, was heated by a huge open fire in the middle of the floor. On windy days the fire filled the whole building with choking smoke as there was only a hole in the roof through which it could escape. The floor was covered with rushes and sweet-smelling herbs which quickly became an evil-smelling mess full of garbage and animal droppings unless the covering was frequently replaced.

There was little furniture: a few trestle tables and benches for the knights and great wooden armchairs for the lord and lady. Of course, as time went by, improvements were made: fireplaces and chimneys were built and more privacy was provided by curtaining off rooms. Although there were latrines, there were still no bathrooms. All drinking water had to be carried from the well. Medieval people rarely washed and wore the same clothes for months on end.

The castle dwellers' food was simple: wheat or rye bread, soft cheese, cabbage and fresh or salted meat. We know very little about castle kitchens but it seems likely that most food was boiled in great cauldrons or roasted on spits. During the long winter months, the salted meat was made a little more pleasant by adding tasty spices from the East. Ale, beer, cider, mead, perry and wine were drunk.

Entertainment was provided by wandering minstrels, jugglers and acrobats. Minstrels were men of importance and went from castle to castle singing, telling stories and providing their employers with the latest news and gossip. Kings and great nobles had their own personal minstrels who poked fun at the proud, self-satisfied members of the courts. Many were men of action. William the Conqueror's minstrel Taillefer opened the battle of Hastings by riding full tilt into the English shield ring and hacking down several men before he himself was killed.

Below left: The Normans built two kinds of keeps: a shell keep and a rectangular keep. Windsor Castle is the most famous shell keep in England while Rochester Castle, shown here, is a good example of a square keep. The bishop of Rochester built a stone castle at a cost of $158 in about 1088 but the present tower keep was erected soon after 1126 by the Archbishop of Canterbury. The entrance was reached by step through a square tower.

Right: A cutaway view through a square keep: 1. Fourposter bed; 2. Fireplace; 3. Arrow slits; 4. Spiral staircase; 5. Chapel and altar; 6. Latrine; 7. Minstrel gallery around the Great Hall; 8. Head table for the lord and his family; 9. Raised dais; 10. Curtained inner door; 11. Guard room; 12. Kitchen sheds; 13. Well; 14. Vaulted cellars; 15. Store; 16. Armory; 17. Dungeons.

The Attackers

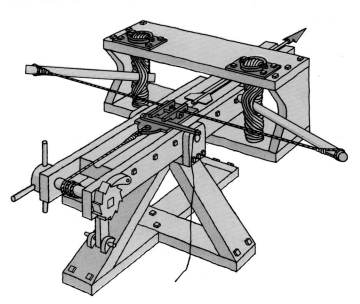

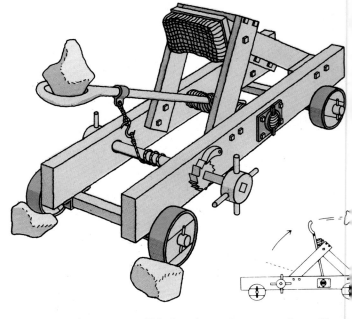

Above: The ballista was the simplest siege weapon. It was no more than a huge crossbow.

Above right: The mangonel was called the wild ass by the Romans. It was a medium range weapon.

Right: Attackers used scaling ladders to climb castle walls a so gain entry.

At first sight, it seems impossible that anyone could have captured a great stone castle, but the attackers found an answer for every type of defence, however clever.

One of the most popular forms of attack was to knock down the walls with huge siege weapons. The most powerful of these was the *trebuchet*. This was a gigantic catapult which threw boulders and rocks. It consisted of a huge wooden framework supporting a long wooden beam with a sling on the long end and a heavy weight on the short end. To use the weapon the soldier pulled the sling and its missile down against the pull of the weight and then released it. As the weight crashed down, the sling whipped up flinging the rock or boulder with enormous force at the castle walls.

The *mangonel* was a smaller but very effective weapon. Its power came from the tension of very tightly twisted ropes. It consisted of a wooden beam with one end hollowed out to take a missile. As the beam was forced downward, the ropes which bound it to its framework were twisted tighter and tighter. As soon as the beam was released, the ropes unwound and the arm flew up, striking the retaining crossbar a

resounding blow and hurling the missile at its target. Being a much smaller weapon than the trebuchet, the mangonel could be wheeled about the battlefield. It was the equivalent of a modern field gun.

An even smaller weapon was the *ballista*. This was like a giant crossbow, and could fire missiles accurately for distances up to 350 or 450 yards.

Although these siege weapons usually flung rocks, they could be adapted to throw barrels of boiling tar or baskets of burning oil-soaked waste, which made very effective fire bombs.

The besiegers used battering rams to smash down castle walls at close range. The battering ram was a heavy beam of wood which could be fitted with a variety of batters, picks and screws. Teams of soldiers then swung the ram repeatedly against the wall until it caved in. Often a ram was suspended from the roof of a *penthouse*. This was a light shed on wheels designed to protect the soldiers working the ram from the castle's defenders.

Another approach was to mine the walls. Penthouses were pushed up to the walls and under their protection the besiegers dug down until they

were under the castle's foundatio While they were digging the tunn underneath the wall they held up roof with wooden pit props. Whe they had finished they set fire to timbers in the hope that the wall would collapse when the supports burned through. Later, in the 14th and 15th century the attackers bl up sections of the wall with bomb filled with gunpowder called *peta*

In the end, the castle had to be taken by assault. Huge wooden s towers, built on wheeled platform and as high as the castle walls themselves, were pushed up to th walls. Once in position, the small drawbridge at the top of the tow was lowered on to the walls so th the attacking soldiers could fight their way into the castle. In the meantime, thousands of other soldiers were propping tall ladde against the walls and attempting climb them while the defenders hurled down great rocks and boil liquids on them. Sometimes, the defenders pushed the ladders awa from the walls with tools like gia boat-hooks. On the other hand, t attackers carried huge hooks call scaling forks with which they dragged screaming defenders fro the castle walls.

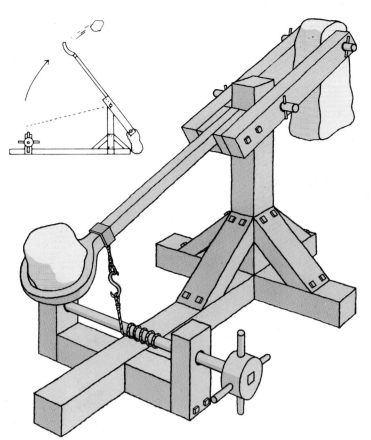

Above: The trebuchet was the most powerful siege weapon. It was remarkably accurate and was used at long range.

Left: The battering ram (so called because its head looked like a ram) needed about 12 men to swing its head against the wall.

Below: Mining was an effective, if dangerous, method of undermining castle walls and causing a breach.

1. Castle wall
2. Wooden pit props
3. Tunnel

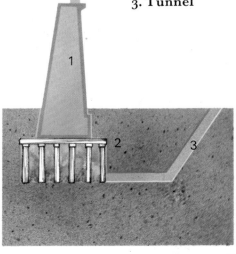

Orders of Chivalry

During the later Middle Ages, the kings of Europe found a new way of binding their knights more closely to them. They founded the various orders of chivalry. The members of these orders took an oath to support each other at all times. Each order had its own gorgeous robes and badges as well as sets of elaborate rules. The word of its Grand Master was usually law. Every so often he held meetings called *chapters*. Although these were ceremonial occasions, kings often made use of them to seek the advice of their nobles. Occasionally, chapters acted as courts of law and expelled knights who had broken their rules or behaved particularly badly, for example, if they were cowardly or betrayed their comrades. The rich and famous were prepared to do almost anything to become members of these exclusive clubs. This would show that they were among the most important people in the country.

During the Hundred Years' War (1337-1453), Edward III of England founded the first order, that of the Garter in 1347. He invited 25 of his finest soldiers to join him. As they took an oath to him as the Grand Master of the order he could be sure that they would never rise in revolt against him and would do everything in their power to conquer France for him. King John of France unsuccessfully tried to counter this move by setting up the Order of the Star in 1351.

In spite of this setback, orders of chivalry continued to be used as a kind of political cement. Philip the Good of Burgundy (1396-1467) whose lands spread all over Europe set up the Order of the Golden Fleece in 1430 to bind his ambitious nobles to him. He succeeded and the Golden Fleece became the richest and most important order of chivalry in Europe. Louis XI of France (1423-83) was so impressed by its success that he founded the Order of St Michael. In this way, he was able to control his unruly nobles and unite France.

Some orders of chivalry spent most of their time fighting the Moslems. The Orders of Calatrava (1158), Santiago (1160) and Alcántara (1166) drove the Moors out of Spain. Before long these three organizations had become so rich and powerful that it was obvious that Spain would never be united until one man succeeded in making himself Grand Master of all three orders. The first Spaniard to achieve this difficult feat was Ferdinand of Aragon (1452-1517) who became king of all Spain.

The orders of chivalry continued to flourish long after the Middle Ages were over. In England membership of the Order of the Garter is still regarded as one of the greatest honors that anyone can receive. Meetings of its members still take place at Windsor Castle, Berkshire, every year.

Above right: Philip the Good, duke of Burgundy who, in 1430, founded the Order of the Golden Fleece, the richest and most famous in the whole of Europe.

Below: The noble Knights of the Garter, led by Queen Elizabeth II and the Duke of Edinburgh, descend the steps of St George's Chapel, Windsor Castle, after a meeting of the chapter.

Right: A painting of the knighting of a member of the Order of the Bath. The new knight wore a blue robe with a white silk lace on the left shoulder. The governors of the order took their leave of the new knight and a noble lady removed the white lace to show that he was a full member of the order. The king and herald watched the ceremony.

A Changing Society

The world of the knight gradually faded away, partly because of changes in the methods of warfare. The invention of the longbow had exposed the weaknesses of the armored knight. This lesson was rubbed in by the appearance of effective hand-guns and cannon in the 15th century. However, it was the use of disciplined pikemen more than anything else which sounded the death knell of the knight. In battle hundreds of pikemen stood shoulder to shoulder in ranks holding spears 15-20 feet long in front of them. The charging knights impaled themselves and their horses on the deadly points.

In this kind of war, rulers wanted professional soldiers, mercenaries who fought for wages rather than gifted amateurs. The decline in the knights' fortunes led to a change of behavior. The winning of personal glory became more important than the protection of the Church or the defence of the weak. Many knights treated the ordinary people with cruelty as well as contempt. This could explain the vicious attacks made on the knightly class during the Peasants' Revolt (1381) in England and the peasants' uprising known as the *Jacquerie* (1358) in France.

Gradually, it dawned on the knights that there was no place for them in the modern world. Some, such as the German knights who rose in revolt against their feudal overlords in 1522, could not accept this and fought to the death rather than give up their ideals and way of life. Others adapted to the new situation and became officers in the new armies. Many poor Spanish knights such as Cortes and Pizarro became explorers.

The ideals of knighthood died hard. Even famous 16th-century rulers such as Henry VIII of England (1491–1547), Francis I of France (1494–1547) and the Emperor Charles V of Germany and King of Spain (1500–58) offered to fight each other in single combat to settle their differences. Unfortunately,

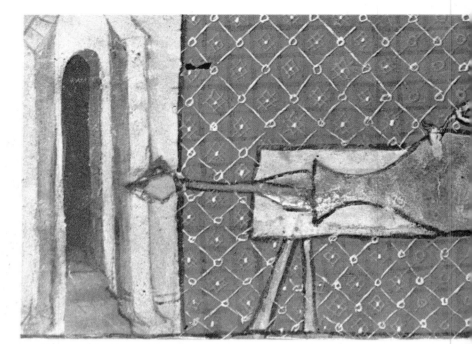